THE TOUCH OF JESUS

The Touch of Jesus

Stewart Jones

Series Editor: James Jones

Illustrated by Taffy

●>> The Bible Reading Fellowship

Text copyright Stewart Jones © 1995
Illustrations copyright Taffy © 1995

The author asserts the moral right
to be identified as the author of this work

Published by
The Bible Reading Fellowship
Peter's Way
Sandy Lane West
Oxford
OX4 5HG
ISBN 0 7459 2576 6
Albatross Books Pty Ltd
PO Box 320
Sutherland
NSW 2232
Australia
ISBN 0 7324 0819 9

First edition 1995
10 9 8 7 6 5 4 3 2 1 0

Acknowledgments
Scriptures quoted from the Good News Bible
published by The Bible Societies/HarperCollins
Publishers Ltd., UK © American Bible Society, 1966,
1971, 1976, 1992, with permission.

A catalogue record for this book is available
from the British Library

Printed in Malta by Interprint Limited

Contents

The touch of Jesus

Who would you most like to meet? Here's a list of famous people. Tick the ones you'd like to spend time with.

- ☐ The Pope
- ☐ Michael Jackson
- ☐ Princess Diana
- ☐ The Queen
- ☐ Mother Teresa
- ☐ The Prime Minister
- ☐ The Archbishop of Canterbury
- ☐ Linford Christie
- ☐ Your country's football manager
- ☐ The President of the USA

Would your life change in any way after you'd met one of these famous people? Sally's favourite film-star was visiting town. He was opening a new cinema. Sally was determined to see him. She waited for hours outside the building. There were hundreds of people there. Sally was near the front. She just knew that he'd see her. Eventually he came to open the building. Everyone screamed as he climbed out of the car. Cameras flashed and everyone cheered. Sally stretched out her hand to touch him as he went past. He stopped to shake hands with people as he walked up the front steps. Sally stretched as far as she could. He was almost at her place. She gasped with excitement as he turned and grabbed her hand. Sally thought she'd faint. He'd touched her. She had held his hand. Sally didn't wash that hand for a whole week!

In this book we'll be looking at people who met Jesus.

Some of them touched him.

He touched them.

But something more amazing happened than not washing for a week!

The way they lived their lives began to change.

Using the code, rearrange the letters and see what changes take place.

```
A B C D E F G H I J K L M N O P Q R S T U V W X Y Z
Z Y X W V U T S R Q P O N M L K J I H G F E D C B A
```

SVZOVW. . . . .

SVOKVI . . . .

ULOOLDVW . . . .

GVOO LGSVIH . . . .

KIZRHV TLW . . . .

As you work through the book why not tick the changes as you discover them?

Being touched by Jesus means change. Change in what we do. How we help other people. What we say. Even how we say it!

The touch of Jesus changed people in the Bible. It can change us, too. As you read through this book, ask God to make changes in your life.

Lord God, as I read this book, help me to be touched by you. To be changed by you. Amen.

2

Spots on your face are a serious problem! Everyone looks at you and thinks you're ugly! No one will ever want to kiss you if you have spots!

Janet had spots. Lots of them. All over her face. She also had a red birth mark across her nose and mouth. Everyone teased her. At school the boys pushed each other into her. The game was: don't touch her! How do you think Janet felt about herself?

. . . .

. . . .

. . . .

Here's a list of different people. Draw a circle around the ones you wouldn't like to be with:

A film-star

A man with Aids

A woman in a wheelchair

A cancer patient

A policeman

A blind girl

An old man

A traveller

A hairdresser

A mentally handicapped boy

Discuss in your youth group why there are some people we don't want to be with.

Read Matthew 8:1–4

When Jesus came down from the hill, large crowds followed him. Then a man suffering from a dreaded skin disease came to him, knelt down before him, and said, 'Sir, if you want to, you can make me clean.'

Jesus stretched out his hand and touched him. 'I do want to,' he answered. 'Be clean!' At once the man was healed of his disease. Then Jesus said to him, 'Listen! Don't tell anyone, but go straight to the priest and let him examine you; then in order to prove to everyone that you are cured, offer the sacrifice that Moses ordered.'

This was a man no one wanted to know. His skin frightened people. They didn't want to catch his disease. So they avoided him. He was an outsider.

Write down in the columns how the man felt before and after he met Jesus:

Before	After
. . . .	. . . .
. . . .	. . . .
. . . .	. . . .
. . . .	. . . .
. . . .	. . . .

Jesus touched the man to heal him. But he touched him to show those watching something very important: this man was accepted by Jesus even though he looked terrible! Jesus made him his friend. It didn't matter what he looked like. Jesus made this outsider an insider of his kingdom.

Is there anyone you know who doesn't belong? What do you think you can do about it?

Jesus help me to try and help

. . . .

[the person you're thinking of]
*feel part of my group of friends.
Show me what I can do to
reach out to them. Amen.*

Ugly friends?

THE
EYE-SPY
BOOK
of
SPOTS

Mrs Clark was a bit unsteady on her feet. She was old and walked with a stick. She was out doing her shopping. Just as she came out of the post office, she tripped.

Her stick went flying and she did too! She fell on her face and smashed her spectacles. The plastic frames were pushed into her nose. There was blood everywhere!

Passers-by rushed over to see what had happened. Some of them stood and watched. Ian, a paper boy on his bike, stopped and knelt down beside Mrs Clark. Her face was a mess. Ian held her hand and said: 'It's okay. We'll soon get you to hospital.'

 **Read Matthew 8:14–15**

Jesus went to Peter's home, and there he saw Peter's mother-in-law sick in bed with a fever. He touched her hand; the fever left her, and she got up and began to wait on him.

Make a list of similarities between the story about Mrs Clark and the story about Peter's mother-in-law:

☐ . . . .

☐ . . . .

☐ . . . .

☐ . . . .

Would you do the same thing?

Tick the actions that Ian or Jesus did which you would do if you were there. What else would you have done?

. . . .

. . . .

Ian acted like Jesus. It's not always difficult to do what Jesus does. Sometimes we make it harder than it needs to be! Often we need to just do it!

Dear Jesus, if I can help someone before they ask, let me be brave enough to just do it! Amen.

Just
do it!

How embarrassing!

Write down three things that have embarrassed you:

1. . . . .

2. . . . .

3. . . . .

The class had been discussing families. What they were like, how many were in their family and so on. The teacher had brought in a visitor. It was the local vicar. He was available to answer questions and to help anyone who had problems at home. No one spoke. Nobody wanted to talk to the vicar!

Alex had been very quiet during the lesson. His dad had left home that week and he didn't know what to do. He was desperate to talk to someone. But the vicar? No way! What would everyone think? The bell went for the end of the session. Everyone got up and started to leave. Alex waited till last. Should he talk to this vicar or not?

What do you think happened next?

Finish the story by completing the pictures in this storyboard:

Read Matthew 9:18–19, 23–26

While Jesus was saying this, a Jewish official came to him, knelt down before him, and said, 'My daughter has just died; but come and place your hands on her, and she will live.'

So Jesus got up and followed him, and his disciples went along with him . . .

Then Jesus went into the official's house. When he saw the musicians for the funeral and the people all stirred up, he said, 'Get out, everybody! The little girl is not dead—she is only sleeping!' Then they all laughed at him. But as soon as the people had been put out, Jesus went into the girl's room and took hold of her hand, and she got up. The news about this spread all over that part of the country.

In the story about the Jewish official and his daughter two people weren't afraid of being embarrassed.

The official went to Jesus for help. He was an important man. He didn't mind looking silly in front of others. He was desperate. He knew Jesus could help. He wanted to save his daughter. Nothing else mattered.

Jesus was willing to look foolish. Everyone thought the girl was dead. They laughed at him when he said she wasn't. He touched her. He didn't mind what other people thought. He knew he could help.

Sometimes we don't do things because we're afraid of what others might think. Our embarrassment stops us. But if we are desperate . . .

Alex needed help. He wanted to tell someone what had happened but . . .

The Jewish official was desperate.

What do you really want to do?

Lord Jesus, there are times when I don't ask you to help me because it's too embarrassing. Please help me to overcome my embarrassment, no matter what. Amen.

I see!

Read Matthew 20:29–34

Anna and Claire were having a great time. This was the best concert they'd ever been to. The band was brilliant. Only one thing was spoiling the evening. A little girl who kept shouting. She kept on and on.

She was becoming a real pain. Everyone agreed and started to tell her to shut up. But she ignored them all. She wouldn't stop. Eventually the lead singer knelt down and asked her what she wanted. She told him. In the excitement she'd lost her spectacles. She couldn't see without them. The man pulled her onto the stage. She saw the rest of the concert from the side. She was thrilled.

If you were Anna or Claire would you have been annoyed (tick your answers):
☐ a lot?
☐ a bit?
☐ not at all?

Do you think the lead singer should have:
☐ ignored the girl all evening?
☐ had her thrown out?
☐ given her what she wanted immediately?
☐ done exactly what he did do?

Do you think the girl should have:
☐ gone and found someone to help?
☐ done exactly what she did do?
☐ left the concert?
☐ waited till the end and then asked for help?

As Jesus and his disciples were leaving Jericho, a large crowd was following. Two blind men who were sitting by the road heard that Jesus was passing by, so they began to shout, 'Son of David! Take pity on us, sir!'

The crowd scolded them and told them to be quiet. But they shouted even more loudly, 'Son of David! Take pity on us, sir!'

Jesus stopped and called them. 'What do you want me to do for you?' he asked them.

'Sir,' they answered, 'we want you to give us our sight!'

Jesus had pity on them and touched their eyes; at once they were able to see, and they followed him.

I DON'T THINK SHE'D THANK ME IF I TOLD HER I'VE JUST FOUND HER SPECS!!

Here is a list of words. Write down which words you think best describe how Jesus, the two blind men and the crowd were feeling before and after the men were healed.

	Before	After
Jesus		
Blind Men		
Crowd		

Foolish   Excited   Questioning
Angry   Listening   Thankful
Noisy   Interested   Accepting
Loving   Ignore   Hopeful
Willing

Jesus was willing to help. But the men had to ask. And they kept on asking! Just like the girl at the concert.

Write down something you want to ask God for:

. . . .

Now keep on asking!

Dear Lord, please come and help me with

. . . .

[the thing you are asking for]
*I will keep on asking till you answer.
But give me what I need
and not what I want. Amen.*

When we need help it's good to know who to see.

Here's a list of problems and names of people who can help. Match up the problem with the person you think could help.

Problem	Person to help
Depressed	Social Worker
Broken Leg	Fireman
Spots	Policeman
Bankrupt	Doctor
Homeless	Nurse
Lost	Lawyer
Head stuck in a pot	Psychiatrist

There are lots of people who can help us with our problems. Which ones would you:

a) Want to see someone privately?

....

....

b) Take a friend with you?

....

....

Read Mark 7:31–35

Jesus then left the neighbourhood of Tyre and went through Sidon to Lake Galilee, going by way of the territory of the Ten Towns. Some people brought him a man who was deaf and could hardly speak, and they begged Jesus to place his hands on him. So Jesus took him off alone, away from the crowd, put his fingers in the man's ears, spat, and touched the man's tongue. Then Jesus looked up to heaven, gave a deep groan, and said to the man, 'Ephphatha,' which means, 'Open up!'

At once the man was able to hear, his speech impediment was removed, and he began to talk without any trouble.

This man had some good friends. They brought him to Jesus to get help. Jesus heals him, but away from the crowd.

Tick the reason why you think he did this:

☐ Because he wasn't sure it would work
☐ Because he wanted to keep the treatment secret
☐ Because he wanted to protect the man from being exploited
☐ Because he didn't like the look of the crowd
☐ Because he didn't want to spit in front of other people
☐ Because he respected the man as an individual

There are things that it is best to keep between ourselves and one other person. This is especially true of personal problems. When we go to see the doctor we don't want all our friends to be in the room at the same time!

The same is true with God. Some things we tell him are between him and us. That's the way it should be. It's the way Jesus helped this man.

Thank you Lord Jesus that when I come to you with a problem you are willing to keep it private. Amen.

HELP!!

PROBLEMS

Phil broke his leg playing football. The pain was terrible. He thought it would never end. He was rushed to hospital in an ambulance where they put his leg in plaster. The next day he was told that it would take nine weeks to heal!

Nine weeks! Phil thought that was forever. He wouldn't be able to play football for nine weeks! Then he realized it'd be even longer than that. The nine weeks was just till the plaster came off. The doctor said it might be another three months before he'd be fit enough to play. Phil thought, 'This is just the end. It's too long. Why does it take so long to get better?'

 *Read Mark 8:22–26*

They came to Bethsaida, where some people brought a blind man to Jesus and begged him to touch him. Jesus took the blind man by the hand and led him out of the village. After spitting on the man's eyes, Jesus placed his hands on him and asked him, 'Can you see anything?'

The man looked up and said, 'Yes, I can see people, but they look like trees walking about.'

Jesus again placed his hands on the man's eyes. This time the man looked intently, his eyesight returned, and he saw everything clearly. Jesus then sent

It takes time!

him home with the order, 'Don't go back into the village.'

Can you find these words from this story in this word search?

```
Z Q A D I A S H T E B
K T U R P P E F O Y H
T M I N G C E K S E S
O N R P A N K O Y S L
H A N D S T I R P C D
C E P E S O R K U L W
U H E Y L R A E L C E
O R X E T A I V N A D
T T O F S Q P R L M W
```

Bethsaida   Eyes   Touch
Spit   Trees   Walking
See   Clearly   Hands
People

To find the words takes some time. In the story Jesus takes a bit of time to heal this man. When we ask God for something we often want an answer immediately. It's hard to wait.

Fill in the following columns. Write down three things you have asked God for. If you've had an answer, write it down. Has there been a time delay? Write down how long.

Requests	Answers	Delay

If you can't think of anything at the moment why don't you start today and complete the boxes when you have an answer. Just because it takes time doesn't mean that God's forgotten. It means that it will be finished in the right way at the right time.

Lord, you know how I hate having to wait. I want answers immediately. Please help me to realize you don't always answer instantly but that you always hear my prayers. Amen.

P.S. A preacher once said that when we pray God always answers. 'Yes', or 'No', 'Not yet', or 'You must be joking!'

What frightens you?

Mark the following things that can be frightening, on our 'Frightometer'.
(10 means heart-stopping fear,
2 means slightly worried!)

Not being able to get a job

1 2 3 4 5 6 7 8 9 10

Failing my exams

1 2 3 4 5 6 7 8 9 10

Having no money

1 2 3 4 5 6 7 8 9 10

Nowhere to live

1 2 3 4 5 6 7 8 9 10

Death

1 2 3 4 5 6 7 8 9 10

Having no friends

1 2 3 4 5 6 7 8 9 10

Being disabled

1 2 3 4 5 6 7 8 9 10

Never having a girlfriend/boyfriend

1 2 3 4 5 6 7 8 9 10

Is there anything else that frightens you?

. . . .

 Read Luke 7:11–15

> *Soon afterwards Jesus went to a town called Nain, accompanied by his disciples and a large crowd. Just as he arrived at the gate of the town, a funeral procession was coming out. The dead man was the only son of a woman who was a widow, and a large crowd from the town was with her. When the Lord saw her, his heart was filled with pity for her, and he said to her, 'Don't cry.' Then he walked over and touched the coffin, and the men carrying it stopped. Jesus said, 'Young man! Get up, I tell you!' The dead man sat up and began to talk, and Jesus gave him back to his mother.*

The mother of the dead man in this story had plenty to be frightened about. She was alone. Both her husband and son are dead. Finding enough money to live on was going to be very hard. There's no one to help her. This might mean she'd have no where to live. The situation was terrible.

Jesus is very upset by what he sees. He wants to help. He raises the man from the dead.

Dead sure?

Jesus is the world's worst funeral director! He spoils funerals he attends, including his own! The story of Jesus dying on the cross and on the third day being raised to new life shows us very clearly that even death is beaten. We don't have to be frightened of it.

Here is the most famous verse in the Bible:

For God loved the world so much that he gave his only Son, so that everyone who believes in him may not die but have eternal life. (John 3:16)

Why not try to learn it by heart?

Look at what you've said you're frightened of. Now say the verse John 3:16 out loud. Sit quietly for a moment. Now say 'Amen'.

Breaking the rules

Tim was in charge of the money from the youth group. Each week he collected the 50p from every member. On his way to the bank he was stopped by a beggar. 'Can you let me have some money for a cup of tea?' asked the man. Tim didn't know what to do. He wanted to help, but he'd always been told not to give people like this any money. And the only money he had belonged to the club. What do you think he should do? (You might like to discuss this in your youth group.)

. . . .

. . . .

. . . .

Now read what happened next:

The beggar asked him again. 'Please help me! I've not eaten all day and I'm starving.'

Tim decided he would help. He told the man he'd be back. He crossed the road and went into the sandwich shop. He bought two packets of sandwiches and a cold drink. He then went back to the man and gave it to him.

The next club night he had to tell the others what had happened. What happened next? Finish the story in your own words.

. . . .

. . . .

. . . .

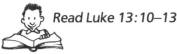 *Read Luke 13:10–13*

One Sabbath Jesus was teaching in a synagogue. A woman there had an evil spirit that had made her ill for eighteen years; she was bent over and could not straighten up at all. When Jesus saw her, he called out to her, 'Woman, you are free from your illness!' He placed his hands on her, and at once she straightened herself up and praised God.

You would think everyone would have been pleased at what Jesus did. But no. The people who were in charge accused Jesus of breaking the rules. The Sabbath was a day to rest. Healing someone on that day wasn't allowed!

But Jesus saw it differently. The woman needed help and he helped her. Tim did the same thing. Do you think they broke the rules? Discuss with your friends what you'd have done.

Lord Jesus, help me never to see rules as the most important thing in life. When someone needs my help, let me put them first. Amen.

> **Extra! Extra!**
> **Have a look at the Ten Commandments. These are very famous rules from the Bible. You'll find them in Exodus 20:17. In your group discuss this question: 'Is it ever right to break these rules?'**

please help

10

Important people

'Go away!' said the man behind the counter. Alice who could hardly see over the desk wanted to talk to the bank manager. 'But I want to talk to him about my money,' pleaded Alice. 'Look I'm terribly sorry little girl but he's far too busy at the moment to see anyone, never mind you!' answered the man. 'But, please can't I just see him for a minute?' asked Alice. 'No!' shouted the man. 'Now go away.' Just then, the manager's door opened. He'd heard all the noise and came to see what was going on.

He came over to ask what he could do to help. Alice explained that she wanted to see him about her money. The manager showed her into his office. The man behind the counter was amazed. He'd never seen a child go into the manager's office before!

Who is the most important in this list? Number them 1–10 with 1 being very important and 10 being least important.

Person	Number
The dustman	......
The Pope	......
Headmaster	......
Mum	......
The Queen	......
A baby	......
A doctor	......
Film star	......
International footballer	......
Next door neighbour	......

 Read Matthew 19:13–15

Some people brought children to Jesus for him to place his hands on them and to pray for them, but the disciples scolded the people. Jesus said, 'Let the children come to me and do not stop them, because the Kingdom of heaven belongs to such as these.'

He placed his hands on them and then went away.

Put a tick beside which of these statements you think best describes how adults treat young people.

- ☐ Don't speak unless you're asked
- ☐ Feel free to say what you think
- ☐ You can do that when you're older
- ☐ Make as much noise as you like
- ☐ Sit still
- ☐ When I was young we had to do as we were told
- ☐ You can't come in here
- ☐ Let's watch what you want
- ☐ I'm too busy right now
- ☐ Let's talk about this

Jesus sees children not as future adults but as people. He loves them as present members of his kingdom. Not just as future members! Young people are as welcome in the kingdom as anyone else. They matter!

Dear Lord, thank you that I'm very important in your eyes. Thank you that I am welcome in your kingdom. Amen.

11

What happened next?

Imagine you're in a time machine. You are taken back to the time of Jesus. You are in the crowd when:

☐ He heals the man of leprosy
☐ He heals Peter's mother-in-law
☐ He raises the dead
☐ He helps blind men to see

☐ He helps a man to hear and speak

Choose one of the five scenes. How would you react?

Here are some things you might do. Colour in the bar to show what your reaction would be. (Colouring a lot means a strong reaction.)

EXCUSE ME... IS THIS FIRST CENTURY PALESTINE?!

TIME MACHINE

Pinch yourself to see if you're dreaming

[ ]

Praise God

[ ]

Follow Jesus

[ ]

Move to back of crowd

[ ]

Tell others

[ ]

Help others

[ ]

Try to work out how it happened

[ ]

When Jesus touched people, some of them praised God, others followed him. Still others helped him and some of them spread the news about him. All four reactions are in the stories. When we meet with God in Jesus, something happens to us *and* makes us decide for or against him.

How do you respond to Jesus? Write down some of the ways you have reacted to Jesus:

. . . .

. . . .

. . . .

Are any the same as the people in the stories? Draw a circle around the ones that are the same. The Jesus we meet is the same today as always. Our reaction to him won't be that different to the people who met him in the Bible.

Lord Jesus, I want to tell others, help and praise you. Just like so many other people. Please help me to do that. Amen.

'Help!' screamed Jim. He was in trouble. He'd been walking his dog, Jake, along the cliff top path and he'd slipped. He slithered down the cliff to a ledge about ten feet below the path. He'd hurt his ankle. He couldn't climb back up. Jake stood at the top barking at him. Stupid dog, thought Jim. Go and get help. He shouted again and again.

Suddenly a man appeared at the cliff edge. He looked at Jim and lay down flat on the ground. He stretched out his hand and told Jim to grab hold. Jim stained every muscle in his body and tried to reach the man's hand. He wished he was a lot taller!

After what seemed like forever Jim's hand touched the man's. He gripped Jim very tightly and started to pull him to safety. It was a remarkable rescue. The man had saved Jim.

DON'T JUST BARK !! GIVE ME A PAW!!

If only...

*WOOF!
WOOF!*

Fill in the columns with words that describe how Jim felt before and after he was rescued:

Before   **After**

. . . .

. . . .

. . . .

. . . .

Read Luke 8:42–44

As Jesus went along, the people were crowding him from every side. Among them was a woman who had suffered from severe bleeding for twelve years; she had spent all she had on doctors, but no one had been able to cure her. She came up in the crowd behind Jesus and touched the edge of his cloak, and her bleeding stopped at once.

Look at the words you put in the columns for Jim. Circle any that you think would describe this woman before and after she touched Jesus.

Like Jim and the woman, there are times when we are desperate for help. So desperate that just a little help is all that's needed. That will make all the difference.

With Jesus that's true. That woman only touched the edge of his cloak and she was healed. A little thing, but look what happened. Jesus can help us when we reach out to him.

Lord, help me to remember to reach out to you when I'm desperate. Help me to know that one little touch can change everything. Amen.

Here's a list of things that some Christians do. Tick the ones that you'd rather not do:

☐ Go to church
☐ Pray out loud
☐ Tell others about Jesus
☐ Read the Bible with other people listening
☐ Sing carols in the shopping centre at Christmas time
☐ Join a Christian club at school
☐ Help at the church lunch club for old people

Happy	......
Embarrassed	......
Worried	......
Laughing	......
Relaxed	......
Frightened	......
Foolish	......
Angry	......
Hopeful	......
Confused	......

Read Luke 8:45–48

Jesus asked, 'Who touched me?'
Everyone denied it, and Peter said, 'Master, the people are all round you and crowding in on you.'
But Jesus said, 'Someone touched me, for I knew it when power went out of me.' The woman saw that she had been found out, so she came trembling and threw herself at Jesus' feet. There in front of everybody, she told him why she had touched him and how she had been healed at once. Jesus said to her, 'My daughter, your faith has made you well. Go in peace.'

List these words from 1 to 10 to show what the woman was feeling when Jesus said, 'Who touched me?' (Where 1 is the strongest feeling, 10 the weakest.)

Some of the things we do as followers of Jesus make us feel like the woman in the story. We'd rather keep it all private. If only we didn't have to go to church, tell others and so on.

The woman wanted to keep her meeting with Jesus a secret. If only he hadn't asked that question, she'd have got away with it.

But Jesus doesn't want to embarrass or frighten her. He wants her to know why she has been healed. He wants to show her how much he cares about her. He wants everyone else to know what he can do.

It's the same for us. Jesus wants us to know what he's done for us. He wants us to know he cares about us and he wants everyone else to see it too.

Dear Jesus, thank you that you don't want to embarrass or frighten me. Help me to see that you want me to know how much you care and for my friends to see that too. Amen.

If only . . . (part 2)

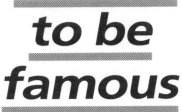

I want to be famous

Would you like to be a famous film star? Or a pop star? Or a footballer? Write down three things that you think would be good about being famous:

1. ....

2. ....

3. ....

Can you think of anything that you would dislike about being famous?

....

....

....

Billy was a singer. He was number one in the pop charts. He couldn't go anywhere on his own. He'd be instantly recognized and within minutes there'd be a crowd of people. They'd scream and shout. They wanted to touch him. To be with him. Billy was famous but was it worth it?

He started to get annoyed with people. Even his friends in the band annoyed him. He wouldn't have anything to do with them except when he was singing. He bought a huge house with a giant wall and guard dogs to keep people out. He didn't want to have anything to do with his fans. As far as he was concerned they didn't matter. He just wanted to be left alone.

He hated being with people at any time. He tried to keep out of their way. Being on his own in his big house was all that mattered.

 Read Matthew 14:34–36

> *They crossed the lake and came to land at Gennesaret, where the people recognized Jesus. So they sent for the sick people in all the surrounding country and brought them to Jesus. They begged him to let those who were ill at least touch the edge of his cloak; and all who touched it were made well.*

Jesus was now famous. He was recognized wherever he went. He had people who wanted to touch him. He didn't get much time to be on his own.

But Jesus didn't build a wall and have guard dogs to keep people away. He didn't want to be alone all the time. There were times when he went away to be on his own. But that was for rest. To be ready for people on another day.

Sometimes we get annoyed when God doesn't sort things out immediately. Sometimes we think our troubles are not worth bothering about.

Jesus isn't like Billy. He doesn't keep out of our way for ever. He wants to help us. But it will be when he thinks that's best for us. Jesus is faithful. That means we can rely on him. If we are following him we need to do the same.

Lord Jesus, thank you that you want me to come to you and to ask you for help. Thank you that you are faithful to me and to everyone who follows you. Amen.

Look and see!

Recently the 'Magic Eye' books have become very popular. As you look at the picture on the page, you can see another picture come into focus. Get hold of a copy of one of the books and try it for yourself. Sometimes you can only see one image until someone shows you how to see the other picture.

Read Luke 24:36–43

While the two were telling them this, suddenly the Lord himself stood among them and said to them, 'Peace be with you.'

They were terrified, thinking that they were seeing a ghost. But he said to them, 'Why are you alarmed? Why are these doubts coming up in your minds? Look at my hands and my feet, and see that it is I myself. Feel me, and you will know, for a ghost doesn't have flesh and bones, as you can see I have.'

He said this and showed them his hands and his feet. They still could not believe, they were so full of joy and wonder; so he asked them, 'Have you anything here to eat?' They gave him a piece of cooked fish, which he took and ate in their presence.

The first followers of Jesus couldn't see that he was really alive. They only saw one thing: a ghost!

They had to be shown how to see things in a different way. Jesus showed them that he wasn't a ghost by eating some fish. He told them to touch him. To feel his body! As they looked they began to change.

It was only as Jesus helped them that they began to change.

Read the story again. Fill in the missing letters below. There's just enough to help you to complete the words. They describe the change in those men.

1. T _ _ _ _ f _ _ _

2. A _ _ _ _ _ d

3. D _ _ b _ _

4. J _ _

5. W _ _ _ _ r

As these men changed, so they saw what was really there. When we want to see what God is doing, we need to change. That is often very hard. But like a 'Magic Eye' picture if we keep looking then we will see things differently. That's how Jesus always wants us to live when we follow him. To see things in a new way. His way.

Lord Jesus, I look at the world around me and I don't often see what you are doing in it. Open my eyes and change me just like you did with your first followers. Amen.

Here are some people and five reasons why you might go to see them. Match up a person with a reason for going to see them by drawing a line from one to the other.

Your Mum
A Policeman   Feeling sick
A Dentist   Help with homework
A Fireman   Lost
A Doctor   Help with finding a job
A Teacher   Stuck up a tree
A Careers Adviser
A Nun

We have been looking at stories in which people came to Jesus. They all wanted help in some way. They all had reasons for coming to him.

Write down some of the reasons you think they came to Jesus.

. . . .

. . . .

. . . .

BUT I CAN'T BE HEAVY — I'M YOUR BROTHER!!

For some it was because they were desperate. Others came because they'd heard about him and knew he could help.

Reach out and touch

 **Read Matthew 11:28–30**

'Come to me, all of you who are tired from carrying heavy loads, and I will give you rest. Take my yoke and put it on you, and learn from me, because I am gentle and humble in spirit; and you will find rest. For the yoke I will give you is easy and the load I will put on you is light.'

What does this mean?

Sam couldn't walk after he'd broken his leg. His brother Ian carried him on his back wherever he went. One day a man saw them struggling up the hill. He said to Ian: 'That's a heavy burden you're carrying there.' And he pointed to Sam on Ian's back.

Ian replied: 'That's no burden, that's my brother.'

Jesus wants us to share our burdens with him. He will give us a light yoke. A yoke is a piece of wood fitted to an ox or cow. This allows the farmer to guide the ox in the fields. They could be very heavy and hurt the animal. Jesus is telling us that he will guide us using a well-made 'yoke'. It won't hurt us, or be too heavy because, like Ian, it will be done out of love. Ian loved Sam and carrying him wasn't a burden. The same is true of the things Jesus asks us to carry when we follow him.

Tick those things that you think are heavy loads.

- ☐ fear
- ☐ anger
- ☐ sickness
- ☐ guilt
- ☐ loneliness
- ☐ joy
- ☐ sadness
- ☐ happiness
- ☐ depression
- ☐ laughter

If there's something that is really bothering you at the moment why not discuss it with your youth group leader, minister or a friend.

Thank you Lord Jesus that you are willing to share the burden of everything that really troubles me. Thank you that I can come to you, touch you, and know that you will help me. Amen.

17

Who's the captain?

I once went for an all night hike. It was wet, cold and very tiring. At one point on the hike we thought we were lost. A mist came down very suddenly and we couldn't see where we were going. Our torches were useless. They only lit up the mist! If it hadn't been for our leader we might never have found our way down the mountain. He was an expert. He knew exactly what to do when the mist came. His careful map-reading and willingness to show us the way was just what we needed. We were all very happy to follow him.

 *Read Matthew 9:35–38*

> *Jesus went round visiting all the towns and villages. He taught in the synagogues, preached the Good News about the Kingdom, and healed people with every kind of disease and sickness. As he saw the crowds, his heart was filled with pity for them, because they were worried and helpless, like sheep without a shepherd. So he said to his disciples, 'The harvest is large, but there are few workers to gather it in. Pray to the owner of the harvest that he will send out workers to gather in his harvest.'*

Here's a list of things you might do. Put a tick beside those you would try without help.

☐ Walking to school
☐ Going to a rock concert
☐ Rock climbing
☐ Hang gliding
☐ A French test
☐ Washing the car
☐ Delivering newspapers
☐ Choosing a career
☐ Tidying your room
☐ Playing the piano

There are lots of things that we need help with. Jesus sees that having a good leader is very important. When he saw the people he thought they were like sheep without a shepherd. Without a leader, sheep get lost. They wander all over the place. They go into dangerous places. They are helpless.

The most important thing we do is the way we live our life. We need someone to help us to do that well. Jesus can be that person. When he isn't, he is deeply saddened. Because without him we're lost.

Lord Jesus, please be the leader in my life. Show me the way and what you want me to do. Amen.

Extra! Extra!
Here's a game you could try with your friends. Find a milk bottle. Have a piece of string for each player. Tie a button or paper clip to the end of the string to give it weight. Put the weights in the bottle and leave each piece of string hanging over the edge of the bottle. On the count of three each player tries to pull their string out. How many people managed to get out of the bottle? Next time appoint a leader who tells each player when to pull. How many were pulled out this time? Having a leader can make a big difference!

18

INTO ACTION

Try this quiz.

1. You see a film on TV about starving people in Africa. Do you:
- [ ] a) switch to something more interesting?
- [ ] b) cry?
- [ ] c) send more money?
- [ ] d) get your friends to do something to raise money for them?

2. You are asked to help with visiting at an old people's home. Do you:
- [ ] a) say you're too busy?
- [ ] b) plan to go but forget?
- [ ] c) think it's a good idea?
- [ ] d) go and get to know one of the people really well?

3. You see a beggar in the street. Do you:
- [ ] a) cross the street?
- [ ] b) feel sorry for them and then cross the street?
- [ ] c) go and get some food for them and give it to them?
- [ ] d) give them some money?

4. You meet a woman who has fallen and cut her leg. Do you:
- [ ] a) tell her where the nearest doctor is?
- [ ] b) run and get help?
- [ ] c) ask her how she did it?
- [ ] d) faint at the sight of blood?

Scores

Q1:	a) 0	b) 1	c) 2	d) 3
Q2:	a) 0	b) 2	c) 1	d) 3
Q3:	a) 0	b) 1	c) 3	d) 2
Q4:	a) 1	b) 3	c) 2	d) 0

My score: ....

 Read Matthew 14:14

> Jesus got out of the boat, and when he saw the large crowd, his heart was filled with pity for them, and he healed those who were ill.

Compare your quiz score to the chart below.

Less than 4: You feel sorry sometimes but so what!

5–9: You feel sorry and you're starting to do something about it!

Over 9: You feel sorry, do something and want to help those who did badly in this quiz!

It's not that difficult to feel sorry for people. Lots of people do. The difference comes in what happens after you felt sorry.

Jesus felt sorry for the people he saw. He did something about it. We need to do the same.

Jesus, when I see someone in trouble show me what I can do to help them.

Amen.

Score out of 10 which of these you're good at. 1 means poor; 10 means very good.

	Score
Volunteering to help at school	......
Washing up	......
Making friends	......
Saving money	......
Playing sport	......
Solving puzzles	......
Explaining things to others	......
Having ideas for things to do in the holidays	......
Listening to other people	......
Writing letters	......

Jesus was very good at helping people. It's what he's always doing. He wants his followers to be the same. But that means there have to be changes!

 **Read Mark 14:45–50**

As soon as Judas arrived, he went up to Jesus and said, 'Teacher!' and kissed him. So they arrested Jesus and held him tight. But one of those standing there drew his sword and struck at the High Priest's slave, cutting off his ear. Then Jesus spoke up and said to them, 'Did you have to come with swords and clubs to capture me, as though I were an outlaw? Day after day I was with you teaching in the Temple, and you did not arrest me. But the Scriptures must come true.'

Then all the disciples left him and ran away.

Describe how Jesus must have felt when all his friends ran away:

....

....

These first followers of Jesus failed. They ran away. They made mistakes. They argued. They didn't understand.

But Jesus didn't give up on them. He wanted to help them. He wanted to change them.

That had to start inside their hearts. Jesus wanted to put in good things and take out bad things. But he only did that with those who wanted it. Judas didn't want to change. Jesus couldn't force him to change.

Find in the word square the kind of things that Jesus put in their hearts:

```
E V O L F K O N T R P Y
S F Y C B J H A E H Q Z
S S E N D O O G M L R H
E L E N T Y I U P C U A
N N H N C K F L G M E D
L P L J D H A D I O C S
U Y N V Q N N L T M N F
F V O E L R I E C A E P
H U U R B T T K J K I H
T X P C Y I Z V F S T D
I S Y I N F M H E M A G
A R L A G Y K U C S P I
F S E L F C O N T R O L
```

Kindness	Humility	Faithfulness
Joy	Peace	Self-control
Love	Patience	Goodness

What can I offer?

As followers of Jesus, we need the same thing to happen to us. It doesn't matter when we get it wrong because Jesus never gives up on us. His heart is full of love for us and everyone who wants him to help.

But if we don't want him to change us . . . he won't.

Lord Jesus Christ, change my heart to be more and more like yours so that I can help other people. Amen.

PLACE YOUR OFFERING HERE

Tom's daily routine was really boring. Wake up. Get dressed. Have breakfast. Go to school. Eat lunch. More school. Go home. Watch TV. Have tea. Do homework. Watch more TV. Go to bed. Sleep. Wake up. Get dressed . . .

Nothing exciting ever happened to him during school term. It was so dull. The same day in and day out.

Till one day, when he was going to school, he saw a film crew making a TV programme. They asked him to be in it. They wanted to know what he thought about drugs. It was very exciting. That day was certainly different.

Read Acts 3:1–8

One day Peter and John went to the Temple at three o'clock in the afternoon, the hour for prayer. There at the Beautiful Gate, as it was called, was a man who had been lame all his life. Every day he was carried to the gate to beg for money from the people who were going into the Temple. When he saw Peter and John going in, he begged them to give him something. They looked straight at him and Peter said, 'Look at us!' So he looked at them, expecting to get something from them. But Peter said to him, 'I have no money at all, but I give you what I have: in the name of Jesus Christ of Nazareth I order you to get up and walk!' Then he took him by his right hand and helped him up. At once the man's feet and ankles became strong; he jumped up, stood on his

*feet, and started walking around.
Then he went into the Temple with
them, walking and jumping and
praising God.*

The lame man was doing his usual
routine. Describe what that was:

....

....

....

But this day was to be different! He was
expecting money. Peter and John
couldn't give him any. But Peter was
brave enough to give him the one thing
he did have. He healed him in the name
of Jesus. The man never expected that!
His whole life was changed.

What did he do?

....

....

....

The power of God can change things
dramatically. Jesus can break our daily
routine in the most unexpected ways!

*Lord God, as I go about my usual
day, surprise me with what you can
do. Amen.*

Just like him

Martin has a younger brother called Sam. He's a real pain. He always copies what Martin does. He follows Martin around. He tries to do what Martin is doing. He wants to play the same games as Martin. But he just gets in the way. Martin is sick of Sam.

'Stop copying me! Leave me alone!' shouts Martin.

'Don't be so mean, Martin,' says Mum. 'He's only trying to be like you.'

'You should be pleased he thinks you're worth copying,' says Dad.

Younger brothers who copy what we do can be a pest. But when we follow Jesus he wants us to copy him!

Here are two stories we've already looked at. Read them and see if you can find three things Peter and John do that is the same as Jesus.

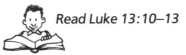

Read Luke 13:10–13

> *One Sabbath Jesus was teaching in a synagogue. A woman there had an evil spirit that had made her ill for eighteen years; she was bent over and could not straighten up at all. When Jesus saw her, he called out to her, 'Woman, you are free from your illness!' He placed his hands on her, and at once she straightened herself up and praised God.*

Read Acts 3:1–9

> *One day Peter and John went to the Temple at three o'clock in the*

21

afternoon, the hour for prayer. There at the Beautiful Gate, as it was called, was a man who had been lame all his life. Every day he was carried to the gate to beg for money from the people who were going into the Temple. When he saw Peter and John going in, he begged them to give him something. They looked straight at him and Peter said, 'Look at us!' So he looked at them, expecting to get something from them. But Peter said to him, 'I have no money at all, but I give you what I have: in the name of Jesus Christ of Nazareth I order you to get up and walk!' Then he took him by his right hand and helped him up. At once the man's feet and ankles became strong; he jumped up, stood on his feet, and started walking around. Then he went into the Temple with them, walking and jumping and praising God.

Three things that are the same:

1. . . . .

2. . . . .

3. . . . .

Can you see any differences?

. . . .

. . . .

. . . .

After Jesus went back to heaven he left his followers to carry on his work. Peter and John were doing just that. As his followers today we should copy Jesus and do what he did.

Discuss in your youth group what you're already doing that is the same as Jesus. Can you think of anything else?

Jesus, I want to be like you. I want to do the things you did so that people will come to know who you are. Amen.

What a change!

John was a thug. He was always causing trouble at the youth club. He broke windows. He bullied other members. He shouted and pestered the leaders all the time. He especially annoyed Alan. He was the smallest of the leaders. John liked to pick on Alan.

One Friday he came into the club but Alan wasn't there. One of the other leaders told everyone that there had been a terrible accident. Alan had been killed in a car crash. John couldn't believe it. He decided to go to the funeral.

At the church he was amazed at the crowds who came. People were sad but they sang hymns and songs as if they really meant them. John couldn't believe what was going on.

The next Friday John went to the club. He walked in and everyone wondered what he'd do. He went to the leaders' office. After a few minutes he came out and started to organize a game of football. What was he doing? Was this just a trick or had John really changed?

Here are some statements. Draw a circle around the number that best describes whether you agree with it or not. (1 means you totally agree; 5 totally disagree)

People never really change

| 1 | 2 | 3 | 4 | 5 |

You don't have to behave differently to be a Christian

| 1 | 2 | 3 | 4 | 5 |

God is only interested in good people

| 1 | 2 | 3 | 4 | 5 |

You can be a Christian without anyone helping you

| 1 | 2 | 3 | 4 | 5 |

God only speaks to people in church

| 1 | 2 | 3 | 4 | 5 |

There was a believer in Damascus named Ananias. He had a vision, in which the Lord said to him, 'Ananias!' 'Here I am, Lord,' he answered. The Lord said to him, 'Get ready and go to Straight Street, and at the house of Judas ask for a man from Tarsus named Saul. He is praying, and in a vision has seen a man named Ananias come in and place his hands on him so that he might see again.'

Ananias answered, 'Lord, many people have told me about this man and about all the terrible things he has done to your people in Jerusalem. And he has come to Damascus with authority from the chief priests to arrest all who worship you.' The Lord said to him, 'Go, because I have chosen him to serve me, to make my name known to Gentiles and kings and to the people of Israel. And I myself will show him all that he must suffer for my sake.'

It's sometimes hard to believe that people have changed. Ananias couldn't believe he had to go and see Saul. The members of the youth club weren't sure about John.

There is only one way of finding out. Shade in the dotted spaces to find out what it is:

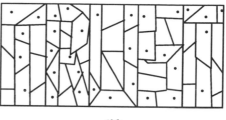

Lord Jesus, when I see people trying to live in a new way help me to believe that the change is a real one. Amen.

WHO WANTS A GAME OF FOOTBALL?!

23

What a change! (part 2)

 Read Acts 9:17–19

> *So Ananias went, entered the house where Saul was, and placed his hands on him. 'Brother Saul,' he said, 'the Lord has sent me—Jesus himself, who appeared to you on the road as you were coming here. He sent me so that you might see again and be filled with the Holy Spirit.' At once something like fish scales fell from Saul's eyes, and he was able to see again. He stood up and was baptized; and after he had eaten, his strength came back.*

What changes took place in Saul's life? Fill in the 'Before' and 'After' columns.

Before   **After**

. . . .

. . . .

. . . .

Saul's life was to change completely. (He even changes his name to Paul!) The change was dramatic and exciting. When God wants something done he sometimes chooses the most unlikely people.

The pictures of the starving children were horrible. Everyone who saw them was upset. People wanted to do something about it. But what could they do? A pop star saw the pictures. He had never done anything for anyone else before. He made money and that was enough for him. But the pictures made him do something. He called all his famous friends and they made a record. It sold millions of copies and made lots of money for the starving.

The pop star didn't think he was the right person to do anything. But God wanted someone to do something and he was the best man for the job.

Saul's life was never to be the same again! We have most of the New Testament to prove that. One thing that must have helped Saul was to be baptized. He did something that showed others and himself that this change was for real. There are other ways of doing this especially if you've already been baptized. Why not talk about baptism and these other ways with your youth leader or minister.

Dear Lord, I want to change so that I am really following you. Show me the best way of making that change last.
Amen.

Here's a list of things you might look for in someone who wants to be a missionary. Give them in order of importance by numbering them from 1 to 10 in the space. (1 is the most important; 10 the least important.)

Number

Good at telling stories	......
Strong	......
Good at telling jokes	......
Brave	......
Someone who prays a lot	......
A good singer	......
Good at languages	......
Can work with other people	......
Can write well	......
Likes to travel	......

 Read Acts 13:1-3

In the church at Antioch there were some prophets and teachers: Barnabas, Simeon (called the Black), Lucius (from Cyrene), Manaen (who had been brought up with Herod the governor), and Saul. While they were serving the Lord and fasting, the Holy Spirit said to them, 'Set apart for me Barnabas and Saul, to do the work to which I have called them.' They fasted and prayed, placed their hands on them, and sent them off.

How were Saul and Barnabas chosen?

....

....

....

They didn't see an advert for the job and apply. God chose them and God told them who was to do the job.

In the first column, write down the names of the people in your youth group.

Name	Jobs to be done
....	....
....	....
....	....
....	....
....	....
....	....
....	....
....	....

Just the job

Now in the second column make a list of some of the jobs that you think need to be done in your group or church.

Pray about who should do which job.
Now draw a line from a name to a job to show which person you think should do the job. As a group, pray about this. Now compare your lists and lines. Who should be doing the jobs?

Heavenly Father, show me what you want me to do for you. Help me to accept the guidance of other people when it comes to doing things for you. Amen.

Some people think they have to do certain things to avoid bad luck. Here are some of them.

Never walk under a ladder
Don't put an umbrella up inside
Don't break a mirror
Don't let a black cat walk past you
Fingers crossed

Can you think of any others?

. . . .

. . . .

. . . .

One that isn't mentioned above is 'touch wood'. Perhaps this is the most common. In fact it goes back to the idea of touching the wood of the cross that Jesus died on. People believe that by touching the cross it will stop bad things happening to them. Some people have a lucky charm. They think that a teddy or a rabbit's foot will help them.

 *Read Acts 19:11–12*

> God was performing unusual miracles through Paul. Even handkerchiefs and aprons he had used were taken to those who were ill, and their diseases were driven away, and the evil spirits would go out of them.

Read the verses again and this time underline the words that answer these questions:

1. What was used to heal people?
2. What were people healed from?
3. Who healed them?

People believed that by touching things Paul had used this would help them. This seems just like having a lucky charm or saying 'touch wood'. But there's one very clear difference. It is God who heals, not the handkerchiefs or aprons! It's important to remember this. Especially when things are tough.

Paul was once in a storm and was shipwrecked. He didn't 'touch wood' and hope for the best. He put his trust in God and he helped him. That's what we need to do in every situation. If we do then God will help us.

Do you have a 'lucky charm'? What do you think it can do for you? What will you do with it now? Why not discuss these questions in your youth group?

Lord God, help me to put my faith in you and not in things that I think are 'lucky'. Amen.

Great faith

P.S. The same thing happened when Jesus lived in Israel. Read Matthew 14:36: *They begged him to let those who were ill at least touch the edge of his cloak; and all who touched it were made well.*

Nowadays you can learn how to do anything. There are lots of books and videos to teach you. How to keep fit. How to play the guitar. How to play football. How to draw and paint. The list is endless.

Read Acts 20:7–12

> *On Saturday evening we gathered together for the fellowship meal. Paul spoke to the people and kept on speaking until midnight, since he was going to leave the next day. Many lamps were burning in the upstairs room where we were meeting. A young man named Eutychus was sitting in the window, and as Paul kept on talking, Eutychus got sleepier and sleepier, until he finally went sound asleep and fell from the third storey to the ground. When they picked him up, he was dead. But Paul went down and threw himself on him and hugged him. 'Don't worry,' he said, 'he is still alive!' Then he went back upstairs, broke bread, and ate. After talking with them for a long time, even until sunrise, Paul left. They took the young man home alive and were greatly comforted.*

I think Eutychus (pronounced 'You-ti-kus') could have done with a 'how to' book! 'How to stay away during a very long sermon!'

Here's a list of words. Put them in the column where they describe how people felt before Eutychus fell, when he fell and afterwards:

Before	During	After

happy	sleepy	sad
amazed	frightened	confused
shocked	bored	fed-up
interested	listening	upset
calm	quiet	noisy
hungry	tired	pleased
relieved	satisfied	speechless

Paul spoke to these people for a long time. All night in fact! He did so because he wasn't going to see them again. He wanted to tell them as much as possible. It was important to tell them how to live as Christians. By raising Eutychus from the dead he showed them that it wasn't just words. This way of life really works! Paul showed that this was how to do it! It is the way Jesus did it.

Our 'how to' book for following Jesus is the Bible. It's full of stories and ways of doing things. We need to learn to put into practice the ways of Jesus. There are lots of things Jesus did. List as many as you can. Tick the ones you've done.

☐ ....

☐ ....

☐ ....

☐ ....

Raising people from the dead doesn't happen very often. That's because there are other ways for God to show us his power. The work of doctors in healing people today is just as amazing as the healings that happened in the Bible. We mustn't try to choose what we think is the best way. Or the most exciting. That's God's job!

Lord Jesus, thank you for the best 'how to' book in the world, the Bible. Help me to do what you did, always. Amen.

ZZZZZZZZ

HOW TO STAY AWAKE IN A LONG SERMON

He's alive!

Carrying on

Have you ever tried abseiling? It's a fast way of getting down a rock face using ropes. It's very exciting. When I learned how to do it I watched the experts first. Then I had a go. I was so frightened the first time that I couldn't do it. I looked over the edge of the cliff and said, 'No way!'

The leader helped me. He took me to a smaller rock face and showed me what to do. I then copied him. Eventually we were able to return to the big cliff and . . . away I went!

One of the best ways to learn is to do what the experts do. Watch them and then copy what they do. The last seven units in this book have all been about that. The first followers of Jesus tried to do what he did.

Here are two lists. One shows what Jesus did. The other one is what we've been looking at. Draw a line to join together the ones that are the same:

Are there any which don't fit together?

. . . .

. . . .

Read Matthew 28:16–20

The eleven disciples went to the hill in Galilee where Jesus had told them to go. When they saw him, they worshipped him, even though some of them doubted. Jesus drew near and said to them, 'I have been given all authority in heaven and on earth. Go, then, to all peoples everywhere and and make them my disciples: baptize them in the name of the Father, the Son, and the Holy Spirit, and teach them to obey everything I have commanded you. And I will be with you always, to the end of the age.'

Jesus	The first Christians
Children coming to Jesus	Peter heals a cripple
Raising a widow's son from the dead	Paul sees again
Healing two blind men	Paul and Barnabas are chosen
Healing Peter's mother-in-law	Healing people through Paul's clothing
Woman healed who touched Jesus' cloak	Raising Eutychus from the dead
Healing a man with leprosy	
Raising Jairus' daughter from the dead	

We need **to go** to the people around us: family and friends. It's up to us to go to them. We need to bring the message to them. We can't expect them to come to us.

We are **to make** them disciples. Followers of Jesus. We do that by getting them to do things with us: helping in a service at church; organizing help for people who can't get out of their house and so on.

We are **to baptize** them. This is usually done by the minister so that it's done at the right time. What it means for a youth group is to make sure that the followers of Jesus stand up in church and tell people that's what they're doing.

We are to **teach them**. Our group should have times when we learn about Jesus. (Using this book is one way!) Playing games is good fun but we need to learn as well.

In your youth group discuss how well you are doing on these four things:

1. How many times have you gone to others to invite them to join in the group?

2. How many people in your group are followers of Jesus?

3. How many people have stood up in church to say they follow Jesus?

4. How many times do you have sessions on learning about Jesus?

Do you need to change anything?

Lord Jesus, thank you for showing us what to do. Help me and my friends to copy what you did. Amen.

IT'S EASY ONCE YOU GET THE HANG OF IT!!

And now...

When Jesus touched people things were never quite the same again. There was a clear before and after.

Fill in the BEFORE and AFTER columns by writing the words that describe people before they met Jesus and then what they were like afterwards.

Healed	Asleep	Laugh
Obey	Praising	Excited
Serving	Frightened	Cry
Run away	Changed	Bored
Challenged	Joyful	Amazed
Lazy	Follower	Dead
Talking	Sad	Doubting

Before | **After**

All the stories in this book show that meeting with Jesus changed things.

Read Ephesians 4:22–24

So get rid of your old self, which made you live as you used to—the old self that was being destroyed by its deceitful desires. Your hearts and minds must be made completely new, and you must put on the new self, which is created in God's likeness and reveals itself in the true life that is upright and holy.

The change that happens in us when we meet with Jesus is as dramatic as changing old, dirty clothes for new, clean ones.

When you change clothes in this way everyone notices. That should be true when we follow Jesus.

Here are more BEFORE and AFTER columns. Write down three things that have changed since you met Jesus.

Before	After
. . . .	. . . .
. . . .	. . . .
. . . .	. . . .

Is there anything else you would like to change?

. . . .

. . . .

. . . .

Ask Jesus to help you make that change.

Lord Jesus, thank you for the changes you have made in my life. Please keep changing me so that I will be more and more like you. Amen.

What next?

The *Following Jesus* Series

If you have enjoyed using *The Touch of Jesus*, you might like to look at other titles in the series. All are available singly or in packs of 10 copies.

Following Jesus—31 units which explore the basics of the Christian faith.

Serving Jesus—31 units which encourage us to serve Jesus in the world today.

Praying with Jesus—31 units which explore Jesus' teaching on prayer.

The Power of Jesus—28 units which consider the power of Jesus as seen in the seven signs in John's Gospel.

Picturing Jesus—28 units which consider the seven 'I Am' sayings in John's Gospel— the pictures which Jesus used to illustrate and show who he was: 'I am the Good Shepherd', 'I am the Vine', 'I am the Bread of Life', 'I am the Way, the Truth and the Life', 'I am the Light of the World', 'I am the Resurrection and the Life', 'I am the Gate'.

Stories by Jesus—31 units which consider ways Jesus used parables to illustrate his teaching and shows how they still relate to and challenge us 2,000 years later.

Surprised by Jesus—31 units which consider ways in which Jesus surprised people by what he said and what he did.

The Spirit of Jesus—31 units which consider the Holy Spirit: the story of the Spirit, pictures of the Spirit and the Holy Spirit and you.

The Teaching of Jesus—29 units consider the teaching of Jesus in the Sermon on the Mount (Matthew 5–7).

Sent by Jesus—30 units which show how Paul, the former enemy of Jesus, became his biggest fan.

The final volume in the series, *The Cross of Jesus*, is in preparation.

All titles in the series are illustrated throughout by Taffy, and are available now from all good Christian bookshops, or in case of difficulty from BRF, Peter's Way, Sandy Lane West, Oxford, OX4 5HG.

If you would like to know more about the full range of Bible reading notes and other Bible reading group study materials published by BRF, write and ask for a free catalogue.